WTF?

What The Feedback

Taking "WTF?" Moments to "WOW!" Results

Kim Baker

Book Cover by 100Covers and Bailey Baack

Edited by Bailey Baack

1st Edition 2026

ISBN: 978-1-968247-76-8 (Digital)

Testimonials

"This is an excellent tool for all managers and supervisors to read prior to giving feedback to employees. There are many individuals that have never had to have these conversations with employees and this book is a great resource. It is an easy read that a person can refer to often for help. I wish we would have had this type of resource years ago." – *Sharon A. Facchin, retired V.P. of Human Resources MECS*

"I read *WTF? What The Feedback* with surprise at how much I needed improvement in both giving and receiving feedback. The book caused me to become more introspective regarding my methods of giving and receiving feedback and has already helped me improve. I strongly recommend this book to all levels of corporate America." – *Jeffrey Hunt Mantel, Ph.D., Executive Director, Technology, Wells Fargo Charlotte, NC*

"*WTF? What The Feedback* is one of the most comprehensive, human, and genuinely actionable guides to feedback I've ever read. It breaks down the emotional realities of feedback — the fears, the triggers, the stories we tell ourselves — with honesty and empathy, while giving readers the practical frameworks they need to become confident and skilled communicators. The COIN model alone is worth the price of the book, but the real magic is in the author's ability to connect skillpower and willpower, helping readers move from awareness to action. This book doesn't teach a 'feedback script.' It teaches a mindset, a process, and ultimately a culture. Whether you're a senior leader, a new manager, or a team member who simply wants better conversations, this book will elevate how you communicate and lead. It's the bridge from fear to fuel, and it delivers on that promise beautifully." – *Judy K. Scheffel, Ed.D., Senior Vice President, CPO, Governance, Operations, Analytics & Transformation (GOAT), Bank of America*

"Feedback is one of the biggest trust builders. It can also be a trust breaker if not done well. This book is a handy guide to help with the will and skill of giving great feedback. All leaders and managers (and frankly everyone that wants relationships with other people) should read and apply the concepts, processes, and tools in this book." – *Jeanet Wade, Expert EOS Implementer and author of The Human Team: So, You Created a Team But People Showed Up!*

"As someone who works closely with business owners, executives, and sales leaders, I see firsthand how poorly-delivered feedback can stall growth and damage trust. *WTF? What the Feedback* addresses that reality head-on. Kim doesn't just explain why feedback matters. She gives leaders a practical roadmap for how to do it well, even when conversations are uncomfortable. The frameworks are clear, actionable, and grounded in real-world leadership dynamics. This is the kind of book that lives on a desk, not a shelf, because leaders will reach for it before important conversations." – *Matt Boisclair, Founder & President, Clear Woods Sales Pathways, LLC*

Acknowledgements

It's only with a bit of luck (I was born and bred not to give up) and these awesome humans that **WTF-What The Feedback™** came about in concept through development of the book, courses, and our WOW! community.

My gratitude goes out to:

Jeff — my forever fiancé. Without you, **WTF-What The Feedback™** could never have happened. Your support when I was spinning multiple plates and facing competing deadlines was fortifying. Your patience when I canceled yet another bike ride because *"I have so much work to do!"* kept me sane, and your love and belief that I could do this when I doubted myself was uplifting and inspiring!

My former spouse and dear friend, "F." Without your support of my early career that came with long hours and travel, **WTF-What The Feedback™** could never have come about in the third and final chapter of my professional life. Thank you, too, for my awesome family-in-laws. I love you all!

Jeanet Wade for all her wise counsel and encouragement in my work, and for being the activating presence for **WTF-What The Feedback™**. Whatever I accomplish professionally is in no small measure due to Jeanet's guidance and mastery! My world is better in so many ways because Jeanet is a part of it!

My inner circle of most trusted advisors. You know who you are! Thank you for taking this journey of development with me. It's with you all that I get to relax, breathe, focus on the inner me, and give to and receive from you.

Our time together is sacred.

The spectacular creatives who helped give birth to "all things" **WTF-What The Feedback™**. Erin Konley — the WTF logo put us on the trajectory for something bigger and better! MaryAnn Russum of Fuzzé Design Group, your energizing yet practical layout of our **WTF-What The Feedback™** course materials welcomes and empowers our participants on their Skwill™ building journey. Jeff Iqbal and Maureen Daley of Daley Design, your insights and creative mastery generated an outstanding website of which I am immensely proud. Dominic Lozano, your enthusiasm and expert partnership from concept to creation and technical feats around the app, QR codes, and assessments were a needed and welcomed lifesaver for this techno neanderthal.

My team from The Skinny: Catherine Jelinek — they say everyone has a book in them, but until I met you, I didn't know that about myself. Thank you for being such an awesome story-writing partner. Bailey Baack — thank you for your calming presence and editing guidance and genius. Ben Heuertz — thank you for your expertise on social media, book publishing, and the role you played in bringing this book to the world!

Those who have presented me with the awkward, icky, sticky, sometimes painful and humbling (yet oh-so-impactful) life lessons, without you I cannot grow!

My clients. You are a source of inspiration, intrigue, and our shared growth. Thank you for your trust in me and for allowing me to take the journey with you as you endeavor to become your next best version of the highest vision you hold for yourself.

Table of Contents

Introduction

Why Feedback Feels So Hard

If you're holding this book, chances are you've had at least one feedback experience that made you think, *"WTF — What The Feedback?!"* You're not alone.

Whether you're a leader, a team member, or an individual contributor, feedback can feel intimidating. It can stir anxiety, activate fears, and shake even the most confident professionals. And the truth is simple: human happens. Feedback touches our emotions, our relationships, and our sense of self. No wonder it's messy.

This book is your invitation into a learning lab, not a perfection palace. A place where vulnerability is normal, skill can be learned, and confidence grows with practice. A place where we cross the bridge from WTF to WOW, and begin to experience feedback not as something to fear, but as something capable of unlocking trust, clarity, and performance. Before we cross that bridge together, I want to share why I care about this work so much.

When I first began managing people, I knew the various models. I knew how feedback was supposed to sound. I also knew the stakes. When I prepared to give feedback, I wasn't afraid of someone crying or storming out. My fear was what might happen after: team fallout, retaliation, misinterpretation, damaged trust.

I'm highly interpersonally sensitive and deeply driven. It's a tricky combination; I wanted to help people grow as individuals *and* I wanted our team to produce high quality work that satisfied our stakeholders. Balancing that was tough for me; I felt the weight of every feedback conversation.

I also had my own share of confusing, poorly given feedback. One moment, my boss told me, *"I think you do a great job — some people think you're a tough trainer."* Six months later, he asked, *"Why didn't you do something about that?"*

"About what?" I asked.

He had never given me anything clear or actionable. He was conflict avoidant. The message I heard was that my boss thought I was doing a great job. I was left to infer, decode, and divine what he wanted from me, which is an experience many of us know all too well. That moment planted a seed in me. I learned that specific, timely, relevant, and honest feedback isn't optional. It's essential.

My background spans sales, global medical device training, talent development, communication workshops, conflict management, and workplace mediation. I've trained thousands of professionals and leaders across industries. I've coached individuals, assessed teams, mediated conflicts, and helped organizations untangle the places where performance gets stuck.

In every environment, the same pattern appeared. Feedback was the pressure point. It was avoided. It was rushed. It was sugarcoated. It was weaponized. Or it was missing entirely. And it always — always — affected trust.

Before COVID hit, I noticed an uptick in client and prospect inquiries centering on low trust. After COVID, I began seeing more conflict, more avoidance, and more emotional intensity in teams. That's when I dove deeper into models of trust, communication, and conflict. I eventually became a certified workplace mediator.

Through everything I've learned, taught, practiced, and witnessed, one truth has held steady: Feedback is the most functional way to build trust... and the fastest way to break it if we do it poorly. That's why this book exists.

Once, one of my direct reports was struggling. She was dealing with something deeply personal, so I held back feedback I knew she needed. I thought I was being compassionate. When I finally gave her the feedback three months later, she asked: *"How long have you noticed this?"*

"About three months," I said.

Her response was, *"I wish you would've told me."*

She didn't thank me for waiting. She didn't feel protected. She felt blindsided. Even with the best intentions... human happens. This book doesn't expect perfection from you. It gives you a path to practice, building your willpower and your skillpower as you learn.

Feedback isn't a routine task. It's not a box to check or a two-hour seminar you attend once. Feedback is a growth accelerator. It's a performance engine. When done well, it strengthens trust, unlocks potential, drives clarity, and gives people the confidence to move faster and perform better. Feedback-rich cultures outperform their peers in profit, trust, alignment, retention, and results. And individuals become clearer, sharper, more capable, more self-aware, and far more confident. They know where they stand. They know how to succeed.

This book guides you through the transformation from WTF to WOW, using the four-stage process we'll build together:

Activate: Assess your baseline. Uncover how your skillpower and willpower around feedback are helping or holding your performance back.

Elevate: Understand the emotional landscape of feedback, reduce triggers, and build the fundamentals of productive conversations.

Accelerate: Develop the SKWILL™ — the powerful blend of skillpower and willpower — that fuels confident, consistent, and constructive feedback.

Perpetuate: Make it a habit. Strengthen your feedback mindset. Build trust on your team. Become part of a community where feedback becomes a cultural advantage.

This book is written for leadership teams, cross-functional teams, individual contributors, people managers, and anyone who wants to work better together. It is accessible, friendly, compassionate, and sometimes a little playful. Because feedback doesn't have to be frightening. It doesn't have to be formal or clinical. It can be a powerful, energizing spark that strengthens connection and accelerates performance for everyone involved.

Across this journey, you'll learn the models, tools, and practices that thousands of employees and leaders have used to build confidence, create clarity, and strengthen trust. You'll grow both your willpower and your skillpower, and discover just how transformative productive feedback can be.

Chapter One

ACTIVATE

Uncover What's Holding You Back

Before you can master feedback — before it becomes energizing instead of exhausting — you have to understand one essential truth: You can't fix what you don't see. Most people think their challenge with feedback is about skill. I often hear sentiments like, *"I don't know the right words," "I don't want to say it wrong,"* or *"I'm not trained."*

But skill is only half the equation. The other half (the half most people never look at) is will. The inner resistance. The patterns. The anxieties. The past experiences. The emotional wiring. The meaning we attach to feedback.

When you think about giving feedback, what comes up first? Joy? Envy? Excitement? Probably not. For almost everyone, giving feedback stirs fear, worry, and anxiety. And guess what? That doesn't mean you're weak or unqualified. It means you're human.

Feedback isn't a mechanical transaction. It's an emotional exchange. So before we can elevate your skill, we begin by activating your awareness and your understanding of what's really holding you back, both when you give feedback and when you receive it.

The Five FEARS of Giving Feedback

We often pretend feedback is "just communication," but internally it's much more personal. Every giver carries fear. These five FEARS show up again and again in leaders, managers, and everyday humans.

FLAK: You worry that giving strong feedback will backfire. What if they quit? What if they get defensive? What if the relationship changes or the conflict escalates? This fear is deeply human: we want harmony, not fallout. And most workplaces don't train people to navigate conflict well, so the fear feels justified. Fearing flak is fearing the immediate negative fallout of giving strong feedback.

EMOTIONS: You may feel anxious before the conversation even starts. You anticipate tears, anger, embarrassment, frustration. And you worry that you won't be able to manage your own reactions, including your tone, your face, your composure.

APPRENTICE: This fear whispers: *"I'm not good at this."* Leaders, especially newer ones, often doubt their competence. They don't want to feel clumsy, unprofessional, or out of their depth.

RETRIBUTION: This fear comes from the political side of workplace life. *"What if they go to my boss?" "What if this damages my reputation?" "What if this creates more problems for me later?"* Separate from flak, fearing retribution is fearing targeted payback from the feedback receiver.

SOMETHING ELSE: Sometimes the real hesitation is hidden. It's not about ability—it's about will. You simply don't want to give the feedback. Maybe the discomfort is too great. Maybe you're conflict-averse. Maybe something about this person or situation brings up old patterns. When the will is low, the skill doesn't matter. Even if you know what to do, you won't do it.

These fears aren't flaws. They're information. And once you can see them, you can work with them.

The Five FEARS of Receiving Feedback

If giving feedback is hard, receiving it can feel even harder. Many people hear the word "feedback" and immediately brace themselves. It's a loaded word.

It often signals criticism, judgment, or disappointment. When someone offers you feedback, it taps directly into your emotional wiring, your history, and your self-concept. Here are the five internal barriers that make receiving feedback triggering:

FEEDBACK: Even before words are spoken, your body reacts. Your chest tightens. Your mind races. You anticipate judgment.

EMOTIONS: Feedback stirs feelings — sometimes big ones. Frustration, embarrassment, sadness, defensiveness, shame. Sometimes the emotion is about the message. Sometimes it's about the messenger.

AWARENESS: Feedback reveals blind spots. It forces you to confront ways you're impacting others that you didn't see (or didn't want to see). This creates discomfort because it threatens the harmony between intention and impact.

RIGID: If you're attached to your habits, your style, or your beliefs about yourself, feedback feels like pressure to change. Rigidity is protection. We cling to what feels familiar because it feels safe.

SKILL: Receiving feedback well is a learned skill. It requires listening openly, asking clarifying questions, managing reactions, processing emotions, and responding professionally even when the message is hard. Most people simply haven't been trained, so the whole experience feels overwhelming.

Understanding the Three Feedback Triggers

In *Thanks for the Feedback* by Douglas Stone and Sheila Heen, three core triggers help explain why feedback can feel threatening, even before we consciously understand why. These triggers help us build empathy for ourselves and others. They also help us develop the *will* to handle feedback with greater clarity and less reactivity.

Truth Triggers

This is the *"That's wrong!"* reaction. Truth triggers get activated when:

- You believe the content is inaccurate

- You judge the data as unfair

- You fixate on flaws instead of potential insights

- You feel misunderstood

This happens because of cognitive bias. We overrate our own abilities. We underrate others'. We judge ourselves by intentions and others by impact. A truth trigger focuses on the content. Not the meaning behind it, not the relationship, just the disagreement.

Identity Triggers

Identity triggers hit the deepest level. They shake our sense of competence, leadership, and capability. When feedback clashes with the story we tell about ourselves, it feels threatening. We may lash out, shut down, or spiral internally, even when the feedback is small. Identity triggers don't show up for everything. You might accept feedback about a report template easily, but react strongly to feedback about communication style, leadership presence, or reliability.

Relationship Triggers

Sometimes it's not about what was said, it's about who said it. Relationship triggers show up in two main ways:

1. Our Opinion of Them

We disqualify feedback if we question the giver's credibility, skill, motives, fairness, or trustworthiness. If we don't respect the person, or don't believe they have authority to tell us this, the walls go up.

2. Their Treatment of Us

Three factors activate relationship triggers:

- Appreciation: *"Do they notice what I do well?"* When people feel unappreciated, corrective feedback feels harsh and unfair.

- Autonomy: *"Do they have the right to say this?"* When feedback feels controlling or intrusive, we reject it.

- Acceptance: *"Do they accept me as I am?"* If we don't feel valued or seen, feedback feels like an attack.

Skill + Will = Performance-Moving Feedback

Performance-moving feedback only happens when both skill and will are present.

SKILL: You know the ideal process. You've been trained. You've practiced. You can deliver feedback clearly, calmly, respectfully, and specifically. When skill is low, you may rely on passive, aggressive, or passive-aggressive approaches. You may avoid or mishandle conversations simply because you were never taught how to do them well. You don't know what you don't know.

WILL: You want to give the feedback. Will is about the emotional, relational, and psychological readiness to act. It is the courage to move forward even when discomfort is present. When will is low, fear leads. You silence yourself to stay comfortable. You avoid important conversations and hope problems resolve themselves.

People with lower will often fall into passive patterns. For them, process and structure — the skill — becomes an anchor that gives them confidence to move. And this is the heart of ACTIVATE: Your FEARS reveal where your SKILL and WILL break down and show you exactly where to grow next.

In your workplace, not everyone starts with the same level of trust, level of training, life experience, cultural background, emotional wiring, comfort with conflict, or willingness to engage. This chapter isn't about **judging** where you are. It's about **seeing** where you are. Because once you see your patterns — your fears, your triggers, your habits — you can change them.

Chapter One Key Takeaways: ACTIVATE

- Feedback struggles are not just about skill. They are equally about will, fear, emotion, and internal resistance.

- Avoiding feedback does not mean you are incapable. It means predictable human fears are at play.

- The FEARS and feedback triggers help explain why giving and receiving feedback can feel threatening, even with good intentions.

- Performance-moving feedback requires both skill and will. One without the other stalls progress.

- ACTIVATE begins with awareness. When you can see what's holding you back, you can change it.

Reflection Prompts

FEARS Exercise: *Giving Productive Feedback*

Reflect on a recent time you avoided or hesitated to give feedback. Which FEARS showed up? Flak, emotions, apprentice (self-doubt), retribution, or something else? What did those fears cost you? What did they cost the other person? What did they cost your team or organization?

TRIGGERS Exercise: *Receiving Feedback Without Defensiveness*

Think about a piece of feedback you received that didn't land well. Which triggers were activated? Truth triggers, identity triggers, or relationship triggers? What did the trigger feel like? How long did that feeling last? What did it teach you about your wiring?

Before we can elevate your skill or accelerate your confidence, we need to begin here, by naming the real barriers that stall feedback in its tracks. You've just taken the first step. You're activating awareness and uncovering what's been holding you back. You're building the foundation that will make every other chapter more effective.

From here, we'll move into **ELEVATE**, where you'll learn to work with your emotions instead of being overwhelmed by them, and build the core skills that make feedback a tool for growth rather than fear.

Chapter Two

ELEVATE

Build the Skillpower

Have you ever watched someone give feedback and thought: *"Wow, they're just naturally good at that"*? If so, this chapter is for you. We tend to talk about feedback like it's a personality trait:

"She's just born direct."

"He says just the right thing in just the right way."

"She's got a knack for knowing when to give feedback."

When we label people that way, we quietly let ourselves off the hook. They are "good at feedback." We… are not. Here's the truth I've seen again and again across teams, leaders, and organizations: **Great feedback is a learnable skill.** You can build it. Your team can build it. Your culture can build it.

This chapter is about skillpower and the concrete techniques that turn feedback from a vague intention into something clear, timely, and genuinely helpful. You'll look at what kind of feedback you're giving, how you tend to give it, and how close (or far) you are from the assertive style that embodies what I call SKWILL-power: **Skill + Will** working together.

The Three Types of Feedback

Before we talk about how you give feedback, we need to get clear on what you're actually giving. In their book *Thanks for the Feedback*, Douglas Stone and Sheila Heen assert that most workplace feedback conversations fall into one of three categories: **appreciation, coaching,** or **evaluation.** When you name which one you're using, things feel less mysterious and a lot more fair.

Appreciation

This is the *"Thank you,"* *"Nice work,"* and *"I see you"* category. Appreciation feedback recognizes effort, contribution, or character and boosts confidence and motivation. It also strengthens connection and belonging

Appreciative feedback can be formal, like awards, shout-outs in meetings, and recognition programs. It can also be informal, like a quick note, a private message, or just a verbal sentiment like, *"Hey, that was really helpful."* When appreciation is missing, people may technically know what's expected, but they don't know if their efforts matter. Over time, that erodes energy and engagement. Appreciation is all positive. It doesn't provoke FEARs for the giver or receiver. Because appreciation is the easiest type of feedback to deliver, the remainder of the book does not concentrate on this form of feedback.

Coaching

Coaching feedback is about growth. It highlights strengths and blind spots, provides guidance on how to improve, and prepares people for new responsibilities and challenges. Coaching is usually more informal and ongoing, often in the form of one-on-one conversations and *"Can I offer you a thought?"* moments.

It is the primary engine of development and performance over time. When coaching is missing, people are left to guess how to get better. They may feel stuck, underutilized, or unsupported.

Evaluation

Evaluation sets the bar and measures against it. It compares performance to standards or expectations and clarifies where someone stands. It also guides decisions about promotions, bonuses, role changes, and continued employment. Examples of evaluation include annual performance reviews, ratings, rankings, and scorecards.

Evaluation has consequences attached. That's why people often feel nervous when feedback is vague. They don't know if they're receiving coaching or something more serious.

When you're clear which type you're giving — appreciation, coaching, or evaluation — your communication becomes more focused, fair, and easier to receive.

Individual Approaches to Giving Feedback

Even if you've never named it, you already have a default approach to giving feedback. You didn't wake up one day and consciously choose it. You absorbed it. It was formed by your family and culture, your early work experiences, the leaders who modeled feedback for you, your personality, and your conflict wiring.

In my two courses, **WTF-What The Feedback™ Giving Productive Feedback** and **Receiving Feedback Non-Defensively**, we organize these approaches along two dimensions: **directness** and **respect**.

- **Directness** – How clearly do you say what you mean?

- **Respect** – How much do you account for the other person's feelings and dignity?

When you combine directness and respect at various ratios, you get four main approaches to giving feedback:

1. Passive

2. Passive-Aggressive

3. Aggressive

4. Assertive

Everyone can learn assertive feedback. Most of us are not there yet. That's okay. This chapter helps you move closer.

The Four Approaches to Giving Feedback

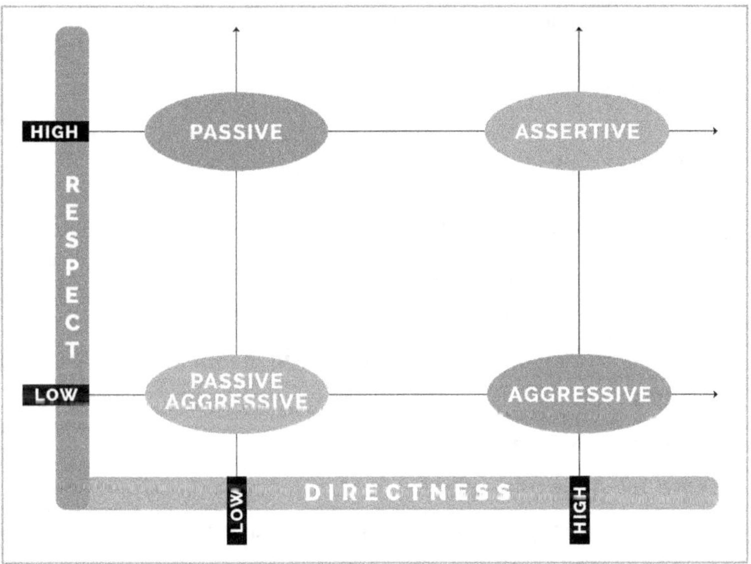

- **Passive feedback** is low indirectness, high in consideration for others, often avoiding confrontation but being polite.

- **Passive-aggressive feedback** is low in directness and low in consideration, mixing in-direct communication with underlying negativity.

- **Aggressive feedback** is high in directness and low in consideration, emphasizing bluntness with little regard for others' feelings.

- **Assertive feedback** is high in both directness and consideration, communicating clearly and respectfully.

Assertive Feedback: *SKWILL-Power Personified*

At the top-right of our feedback quadrant is assertive feedback. **High direct-ness. High consideration.** Assertive givers:

- Are clear, honest, and specific

- Are respectful, steady, and human

- See feedback as an act of support, not punishment

No one arrives here by accident. Assertive feedback is built through practice, reflection, tools (like the COIN model, which we will cover later in this book), and a willingness to do something uncomfortable because it matters.

Think of it as SKWILL-power in action: **Skill in how you structure the conversation**

+ Will to actually have it

When you give feedback assertively, you see feedback as an active way to help people grow, not just a checkbox or HR requirement. Focus on specific, observable actions, so what you say feels concrete and fair. Give feedback promptly, so it still connects to what actually happened. Keep it relevant to the person's role, goals, and performance. Treat it as a two-way conversation, inviting questions, dialogue, and clarity.

This is the "sweet spot" we're aiming for. Not perfect, but purposeful.

Why Assertive Feedback Works

The overall upside to assertive feedback is that openness between the giver and the receiver increases. People feel supported instead of attacked, so defensiveness goes down. Clarity also strengthens. Focusing on behaviors reduces misunderstandings and builds trust. Real-time feedback helps people adjust quickly, creating more efficient results. Tying feedback to goals makes it meaningful and worth acting on. Dialogue invites people to own their development, not just comply.

As the giver of assertive feedback, you experience more purpose because you're actively helping others grow. Your own clarity improves as you describe behaviors and results instead of making it personal. Feedback gets easier because you give it when it's fresh, not after three months of tension. You appear more professional because you keep the focus on performance and impact. Trust grows, because people see you as both honest and invested in their success.

The receiver of assertive feedback will feel more open because feedback is framed as growth, not blame. They gain clarity on what to keep doing and what to adjust. They see the relevance to their role and career, so it feels fair and actionable. They benefit from timely input, making it easier to connect the conversation to real situations.

This is the skill set we're growing in this chapter. But most people don't start with an assertive approach. Let's go over the three non-assertive approaches to giving feedback.

Giving Passive Feedback

Low directness. High consideration. Someone with a passive approach to giving feedback may feel uncomfortable and stressed about giving feedback. They may hesitate even when someone asks for their perspective. When giving feedback, they may soften their words so much that the message gets blurred. They often hope problems will resolve themselves if they wait long enough.

The overall downside of passive feedback is that problems usually persist or worsen. People don't have clarity on what needs to change. Trust erodes because people aren't sure where they stand, so growth stalls for both individuals and the team as a whole.

The cost to the giver of passive feedback includes rising stress as they carry unresolved concerns and rising frustration as the same issues repeat. Their credibility may take a hit when they avoid hard conversations. Ultimately, they miss opportunities to positively influence others and the work.

The cost to the receiver of passive feedback includes growing confusion about expectations and performance and weakening trust if they expect the giver is "holding back." They miss out on coaching that could help them succeed. Engagement and motivation decline because nothing is being addressed.

Giving Passive-Aggressive Feedback

Low directness. Low consideration. Someone who gives passive-aggressive feedback might avoid giving direct feedback even when they are frustrated. They signal their dissatisfaction through tone, sarcasm, or joking jabs. For example, they may often make comments like, *"Nice of you to join us on time today."* They might vent about one person to another, instead of speaking to the person directly. They may also ask someone else to deliver their feedback for them.

The overall downside to giving passive-aggressive feedback is that misunderstandings multiply because the real issue is never plainly named. Trust erodes as people sense negativity without clarity. Resentment builds on all sides and relationships suffer.

The cost of passive-aggressive feedback to the giver is that your concerns remain un-addressed and your frustration lingers, since problems are rarely resolved or improved. Over time, avoiding open feedback increases your emotional strain and leaves you feeling isolated, which lowers your sense of satisfaction and connection in working relationships

The cost of passive-aggressive feedback to the receiver includes confusion about what is really wrong or how to fix it, stalled development because there's no clear guidance, and eroding trust as tension rises and communication stays murky. Without explicit feedback, the receiver struggles to know what to change, hampering growth and progress.

Giving Aggressive Feedback

High directness. Low consideration. Someone who gives aggressive feedback might deliver feedback in a forceful way. They emphasize mistakes and what went wrong while leaning on their title or authority to gain compliance. They may take pride in being blunt and "telling it like it is." They might even drift into personal or offensive language.

The overall downside to aggressive feedback is that fear replaces motivation. When feedback feels like an attack, trust breaks down. People may comply in the short term but rarely take real ownership. Engagement may fall as people withdraw, hide mistakes, or stop taking risks.

The cost of giving aggressive feedback includes the erosion of the influence of the giver; people may tune them out or avoid them. Respect and trust weaken over time. The giver receives compliance, not commitment. They end up more isolated from real information and honest input.

The cost of aggressive feedback to the receiver includes a stall in growth because they are too busy defending themselves. Their confidence erodes as the feedback feels like a judgment of their worth. Trust fades and emotional fatigue sets in, reducing creativity and resilience.

The COIN Model: From Default to Deliberate

If you see yourself in any of those non-assertive styles, you're not alone. These are learned patterns. The good news is that you can learn new ones. One of the most powerful tools we use in **WTF-What The Feedback™** is the **COIN model** for feedback. At a high level, COIN helps you structure your message around:

1. **CONTEXT** – When and where did this happen?

2. **OBSERVATION** – What exactly did you see or hear?

3. **IMPACT** – What effect did it have on people, results, or the work?

4. **NEXT STEPS** – What do we want to see going forward?

COIN supports assertive feedback by keeping you grounded in facts and observable behaviors. When thinking about what is an observable behavior, think of a video camera. Observable behaviors are external behaviors that can be seen or heard on a recording. They aren't abstract or internal, like "being respectful" or "assuming positive intent."

COIN reduces the emotional "heat" in the way you speak, making your message specific, fair, and actionable. Furthermore, it creates a natural opening for dialogue. **Think of COIN as skillpower in a toolbox. It gives your willpower something solid to work with when the conversation feels tough.** Our brains often interpret criticism as a threat, even when the giver is calm and well-intentioned. We also remember negative information more vividly than positive input, which means criticism tends to "stick" and replay. This is why we spent time in Chapter One on truth, identity, and relationship triggers. When you understand these, you can bring more empathy to how you give feedback and make more sense of how you receive it.

Now let's look at four common reactions people have when feedback lands.

The Four Reactions to Receiving Feedback

When someone receives feedback, two things vary: **how accepting they are of the feedback (low to high)** and **how vocal they are about their reactions (quiet to expressive)**. Those two dimensions create four responses:

1. Actively Accepts

2. Passively Accepts

3. Actively Rejects

4. Passively Rejects

You may recognize yourself in more than one of these, depending on the situation and who's giving the feedback.

Actively Accepts

The attitude of someone who actively accepts feedback is, *"I see feedback as a gift that helps me grow, even when it's uncomfortable."* People who actively accept feedback seek the feedback and invite input. They show a clear growth mindset, see mistakes as learning opportunities, and stay persistent even when feedback is challenging.

When working with those who actively accept feedback, be ready with meaningful input; they will ask for it. They are your feedback enthusiasts. Make feedback a regular part of your check-ins. Remember to pace yourself; focus on one or two priorities at a time so they don't get overwhelmed.

Passively Accepts

The attitude of someone who passively accepts feedback is, *"I see feedback as something I should agree with, but I'm not sure it will really change what I do."* People who passively accept tend to be quieter and less overtly expressive. They often show open body language with limited verbal response; they may nod or voice agreement without many questions. They reveal whether the feedback "landed" later, through their actions.

When working with someone who passively accepts feedback, acknowledge their willingness to improve. Co-create a simple action plan with clear steps and follow up intentionally to see what's working and where they need support. Reinforce progress quickly when you see changes.

Actively Rejects

The attitude of someone who actively rejects feedback is, *"I see feedback as criticism and I feel like I have to defend myself from it."* People who actively reject will push back openly, sometimes intensely. They will argue about the content of your feedback, their interpretation of it, or your motives for giving it. They may show defensive body language or use a sharper tone of voice; they might use denial, justification, blaming, minimizing, or evasion.

When working with someone who actively rejects feedback, it's important to stay calm. Don't get hooked into a debate. Check your own process: Was your feedback clear, specific, and fair? Seek to understand the resistance. Do they feel attacked, or do they genuinely disagree? Reinforce your intent. You're trying to help them succeed. Ask curiosity-based questions (*"Can you help me understand your perspective?"*) and listen fully. If needed, pause and agree to revisit the conversation once emotions cool.

Passively Rejects

The attitude of someone who passively rejects feedback is, *"I see feedback as optional so I listen politely, but I don't feel it really applies to me."* People who passively reject may give minimal verbal response, show closed or distant body language, and show little or no change afterward.

When working with someone who passively rejects feedback, gently explore what might be driving their hesitation. Check in respectfully: *"I sense some hesitation. Would you say that's accurate?"* Ask what concerns they have about applying the feedback. Increase accountability with follow-up conversations. Model openness by asking for feedback yourself and showing how you use it.

At this point, you've seen the full landscape of your feedback world—the three types of feedback you give (appreciation, coaching, evaluation), the four approaches you may use (passive, passive-aggressive, aggressive, assertive), and the four reactions people have when receiving feedback. This is your skillpower map.

You now have language to describe what kind of feedback you're giving, how you're delivering it, and how others are likely to receive it. And with that awareness, you can choose your approach on purpose. From here, you're ready to elevate your practice intentionally, consistently, and with the clarity that fuels real confidence.

Chapter Two Key Takeaways: ELEVATE

- Great feedback is not a personality trait. It is a learnable skill that improves with structure, practice, and intention.

- Not all feedback is the same. Clarifying whether you are giving appreciation, coaching, or evaluation makes feedback fairer and easier to receive.

- How feedback lands depends not only on how it is given, but on how it is received. People tend to respond in one of four reactions: Actively Accepts, Passively Accepts, Actively Rejects, or Passively Rejects.

- Assertive feedback — high directness and high consideration — is the goal. It supports growth, builds trust, and reduces defensiveness.

- Tools like the COIN model turn feedback from reactive to deliberate by grounding conversations in observable behavior and impact.

Action Step: *Assess Your Baseline*

Inside the **WTF-What The Feedback™** course experience, we don't just talk about feedback in theory. We start with baseline assessments so you can see where you are today. For this action step, complete the two assessments by scanning the QR code below:

These assessments are your starting point for SKWILL-power. In the next chapter, we'll move into **ACCELERATE**: applying these skills in real situations so that feedback becomes a reliable engine of performance, not a dreaded event. You've named your patterns. You've mapped your styles. Now we'll put your skillpower to work.

Chapter Three

ACCELERATE

Apply, Practice, and Integrate

By now, you've done some important work. You've activated your awareness and elevated your skillpower. But here's the catch: Awareness alone doesn't build mastery. Learning alone doesn't build confidence. Confidence comes from consistent action; it comes from doing the reps. This chapter is about turning what you know into what you do, turning theory into skill, and turning skill into confidence.

Let's walk through the Ideal Process for giving feedback, layer in the COIN Framework, and look at how to receive feedback non-defensively. This is where everything begins to click.

The Ideal Process for Giving Feedback

Giving productive feedback is not a single moment. It's a process that starts before the conversation, continues during it, and carries forward after. This process supports fairness, clarity, emotional regulation, alignment, accountability, and growth.

When you follow the Ideal Process, you remove guesswork and reduce angst for both you and the receiver. It gives you structure, stability, and a repeatable rhythm you can rely on, especially when emotions run high. Let's walk through each stage.

Before the Feedback Conversation

This is the foundation and the part most people skip. When people avoid feedback, freeze in the moment, or get emotionally derailed, it's usually because they didn't prepare themselves first.

1. **Prepare Yourself:** Check your motivation. Ask yourself, *"Am I giving this feedback to support improvement and growth?"* If the answer is yes, proceed. If your motivation sounds more like: *"I'm frustrated and need to vent." "I want to prove I'm right." "I just need to get this off my chest."* It's time to pause. Reconsider. Feedback that isn't anchored in growth usually leads to defensiveness, damage, or distrust. Manage your emotions. If you feel angry, hurt, or activated, take the time to cool down and regroup. Emotional regulation is not a weakness. It's a core leadership skill. It's what allows you to stay steady when someone else is losing balance.

2. **Clarify the Context:** Name the primary type of feedback you're giving — appreciation, coaching, or evaluation. This matters because each type needs a different preparation, tone, level of detail, and follow-up. Clarifying the context also helps you anticipate resistance. If the feedback carries real consequences (evaluation), you need to be especially clear, structured, and fair.

3. **Define the Outcome:** Ask yourself, *"What do I want this feedback to achieve?"* Be as specific as you can. Are you looking for changed behavior? Improved performance? Clear alignment on expectations? A plan or agreement for next steps? Clarity now prevents confusion later.

4. **Prepare for Triggers:** Remember the three feedback triggers. **Truth** – *"That's wrong."* **Relationship** – *"I don't trust you or your*

motives." **Identity** – *"This threatens who I believe I am."* These reactions are normal. Expect them. When you anticipate triggers, you're more likely to stay grounded instead of getting pulled into the reaction.

5. **Choose the Right Setting:** Whenever possible, schedule a private, uninterrupted conversation. If feedback must be immediate, deliver it privately and respectfully. The environment speaks before you do. A private, calm space makes feedback safer to hear.

During the Feedback Conversation

This is the moment most people dread and the one that offers the greatest opportunity for trust and growth. This is where structure matters most. To reduce stress and increase clarity, use the COIN Framework. It gives you a step-by-step way to communicate that is clear, behavior-based, respectful, action-oriented, and consistent. Think of COIN as your "script skeleton." You bring your own voice. The structure keeps you grounded.

The COIN Framework: *Anatomy of Productive Feedback*

C — Context: Set the stage. Be upfront about the purpose. Don't bury the feedback inside small talk. Don't ambush someone without warning. Example: *"I'd like to share some observations based on what I've noticed in our software implementation review meetings."*

O — Observation: Describe exactly what you saw or heard. Stick to behaviors, not personality. Stay neutral, specific, and objective. Instead of *"Your attitude is negative,"* say, *"In our last three meetings, your first response to new ideas has consistently been a negative comment, such as, 'That won't work.'"* Observations give people something concrete to work with.

I — Impact: Explain why it matters. The impact can be on the work, the team, results, relationships, or the person's reputation or career path. Examples: *"When you dismiss ideas quickly, others become reluctant to share. It slows our progress and affects morale."* Or, *"This impacts your own growth, because collaboration is a key factor in the promotion you're working toward."* Impact answers the question, *"Why should I care?"*

N — Now / Next Steps: This is where you shift into dialogue and action. Invite their perspective, discuss solutions, co-create next steps, and confirm agreements. This is where commitment and accountability crystalize. Start with curiosity:

- *"What are your thoughts on what I've shared?"*

- *"Do you see how this impacts the team?"*

Then collaborate:

- *"What steps do you think would help?"*

- *"What support do you need from me?"*

Finally, confirm:

- Actions

- Timelines

- Check-in cadence

Applying COIN: *A Full Example*

Context: *"I want to share some observations I have about your interactions with others during our software implementation review meetings."*

Observation: *"I'm noticing that your first response to suggestions is often negative. For example, at our last meeting, when Cheryl proposed breaking into* *subgroups, you said, 'It would be a complete waste of time.' She shut down after that, and she's usually very engaged."*

Impact: *"When members feel that you are quick to shut down their input, the team hesitates to share ideas. It slows our progress and affects morale. It also impacts your leadership credibility as you aim for promotion, because collaboration is a key expectation for that role."*

Now / Next Steps: *"What are your thoughts on what I've shared?"* Then, *"Let's talk about ways you might respond with questions or alternatives instead of immediate rejection. For instance, you could ask, 'Tell me more about how you see that working,' or offer, 'Could we try a shorter version first?'"* Together, you agree on specific behaviors to practice and when you'll follow up.

Aligning Message and Delivery

Your words matter, but your delivery carries just as much weight. To reinforce clarity, match your body language to your message. Make appropriate eye contact, keep your tone calm and steady, and avoid sarcasm or "joking" at the receiver's expense.

Steer clear of personal attacks, labels, or absolutes like "always" and "never." Do not psychoanalyze or try to guess motives, e.g. *"You don't care about this team."* You are there to describe behavior and impact, not to define who someone is.

Avoid the "praise sandwich" as it confuses the message and feels insincere. A "praise sandwich" is an ineffective feedback method where you give a compliment, slip in the real critique, then close with another compliment. This approach dilutes the core message and makes the constructive point less effective.

After the Feedback Conversation

This is the part most leaders forget. But follow-through is where change is sustained.

1. **Maintain Follow-Through:** Feedback is not a one-and-done event. Consistency builds trust, accountability, and momentum. If you never mention the feedback again, you send a quiet message that it wasn't that important and you reduce the likelihood that real change will occur.

2. **Schedule Check-Ins:** Review progress on actions, behaviors, and expectations. Use check-ins to reinforce growth, remove barriers, clarify expectations, and re-align if needed. These don't have to be long meetings. Five focused minutes can be powerful.

3. **Refine as Needed:** If improvement hasn't happened, revisit the shared understanding. Restate the expectations and explore obstacles together.
   You're not trying to "catch" them. You're coaching them. Sometimes the barrier is skill. Sometimes it's will. Sometimes it's something in the system that needs adjustment. Stay curious.

4. **Reinforce Improvement:** Recognize even small improvements. Reinforcement builds motivation, confidence, momentum, and engagement. When people feel seen for their growth, they keep growing.

The Ideal Process for Receiving Feedback Non-Defensively

Just like when giving feedback productively, receiving feedback non-defensively begins before the conversation ever takes place. At the forefront of the Ideal Process, the receiver takes an active role in navigating the feedback experience — before, during, and after — by advocating for themselves. This does not mean controlling the conversation or avoiding difficult input. It means creating the conditions that allow you to receive feedback thoughtfully rather than reactively.

Before Receiving Feedback

1. **Prepare Yourself:** Before receiving feedback, pause and prepare. This preparation is about clarity, not rehearsing a defense. Ask yourself, *"Am I in a state where I can listen, stay regulated, and think clearly?"* If not, preparation may include requesting a different time, setting expectations, or asking clarifying questions before the feedback begins.

2. **Clarify the Context:** One of the most common reasons feedback conversations go poorly is that the receiver does not know what kind of feedback they are receiving. Before the conversation (or at the very beginning) determine whether the feedback is: Appreciation (recognition and reinforcement), Coaching (development, learning, or improvement), Evaluation (assessment against expectations or standards). Each type of feedback serves a different purpose. Knowing which one you are receiving helps you listen accurately and respond appropriately.

3. **Define the Outcome:** Feedback conversations are more productive when both parties are clear about what they want to accomplish. Before receiving feedback, consider: What do I want to get out of this conversation? What might the giver want to accomplish? If the giver's desired outcome is not known in advance, it is imperative to

capture it at the beginning of the conversation. A simple question such as, *"What are you hoping comes from this feedback?"* can immediately reduce confusion and defensiveness.

4. **Prepare for Your Triggers:** Receiving feedback can activate emotional responses before you even realize it. Before the conversation, reflect on whether this feedback might trigger truth triggers (disagreement with the content), identity triggers (threat to how you see yourself), relationship triggers (reaction to who is giving the feedback). Preparing for triggers does not mean trying to eliminate them. It means recognizing that they may arise so you are less likely to be blindsided by them in the moment.

5. **Choose the Right Setting:** As the receiver, advocate for conditions that support productive dialogue, like a time of day when you are most focused, a location that feels private and appropriate, and a day of the week that allows for reflection rather than rush. If the setting is not conducive to receiving feedback well, it is reasonable and responsible to request an alternative.

During Receiving Feedback

This is where preparation is tested. This is the moment when emotion, interpretation, and communication all converge. The receiver's job is not to decide immediately whether the feedback is right or wrong, but to keep the conversation productive and grounded in clarity.

1. **Clarify the Giver's Intention:** If it has not already been stated, clarify whether this is a feedback conversation. If it is, identify the giver's desired outcome. Clarifying intention early prevents misunderstanding and reduces the likelihood of defensiveness later in the conversation.

2. **Communicate Clearly and Objectively:** As the receiver, your role is to engage in clear, objective communication. This means listening without interrupting, asking clarifying questions, and avoiding assumptions about intent. This also means focusing on observable behaviors and outcomes rather than interpretations. Objectivity keeps the conversation grounded in facts and impact rather than emotion or inference.

3. **Manage Your Emotions and Triggers:** Feedback can activate truth, identity, or relationship triggers in real time. During the conversation, monitor physical reactions (tightness, urgency, withdrawal), emotional responses (defensiveness, shame, irritation), and behavioral impulses (explaining, justifying, dismissing). Managing triggers does not mean suppressing emotion. It means recognizing it and choosing not to let it control your response.

4. **Confirm the Impact of Your Actions or Behaviors:** Ensure you understand the impact being described. This includes the impact on you personally (*"What does this mean for me?"*), the team or organization, and the results, performance, or outcomes. Confirming impact helps you move from vague feedback to actionable understanding.

5. **Determine the Nature of the Request:** Not all feedback carries the same level of expectation. Clarify: Are the suggestions being offered optional, meaning you can take or leave them? Or are they expectations or requirements? If you choose not to act on the feedback or decline the suggested actions, clarify what the expected outcome or consequence would be. This distinction prevents unspoken assumptions and future conflict.

6. **Set and Manage Boundaries and Expectations:** Receiving feed-

back non-defensively does not require immediate agreement or commitment. Leverage processing time when needed. This includes being clear about what actions you are willing to take, what outcomes are realistic, what support or resources you may need, and what timeline makes sense. Pausing to reflect supports responsible decision-making.

7. **Collaborate on Solutions:** When appropriate, collaborate with the giver to identify next steps. State your overall course of action and proposed timeline. Collaboration increases shared ownership and alignment.

8. **Confirm Agreements:** Before the conversation ends, confirm what has been agreed upon regarding actions, expectations, timelines, and follow-up. Clear agreements reduce confusion and prevent future defensiveness.

9. **Avoid Ineffective Approaches and Reactions:** Throughout the conversation, intentionally avoid ineffective responses such as denial, passive acceptance without intention to act, and passive or active rejection without clarification. Set your mindset, manage your triggers, and stay engaged in the process, even when the conversation is uncomfortable.

After Receiving Feedback

Receiving feedback non-defensively does not end when the conversation ends. The "after" phase is where credibility, trust, and growth are either reinforced or eroded. This stage is about execution, reflection, and course correction.

1. **Maintain Follow-Through:** Once agreements have been made,

follow-through matters. Act on the commitments you stated during the feedback conversation. This includes honoring actions, behaviors, and timelines that were agreed upon. Follow-through signals ownership and demonstrates that the feedback conversation had the desired impact.

2. **Attend Check-Ins:** Check-ins are not optional add-ons. They are a critical part of the Ideal Process. Use scheduled or informal check-ins to review progress, confirm alignment, and surface challenges early. These conversations help prevent small issues from turning into missed expectations or defensiveness later.

3. **Refine as Needed:** If you are not meeting your commitments, do not wait for the next formal review to address it. Pre-plan check-in conversations to ask for refinement, renegotiate expectations, or recommit to adjusted actions or timelines. Refinement is not failure. It is a responsible response when conditions, capacity, or information change.

4. **Ask for Support and Remove Barriers:** Improvement often requires support beyond individual effort. If progress is stalled, explore what is getting in the way: Do you need additional resources? Is there a skills gap that requires support? Are there barriers outside your authority or autonomy? Lean on your manager to help remove obstacles that you cannot remove on your own. If the support you initially received is not adequate, ask for refined or different support.

5. **Reinforce Your Commitment to Improvement:** Close the loop by restating your commitment. Confirm any new or refined actions, expectations, and timelines. Reinforcing commitment builds trust and keeps the feedback process active rather than episodic.

Skillpower → Willpower → Confidence

As you continue practicing, your skillpower gives your willpower something firm to stand on. And your willpower gives your skillpower the energy and courage to be applied. Together, they build confidence. This is the acceleration phase. This is where you become someone who:

- Steps into difficult conversations

- Communicates clearly and respectfully

- Strengthens relationships through honesty

- Coaches with clarity and compassion

- Drives performance and trust across your team

This is the heart of WTF → WOW.

The Information Fallacy

Most people assume feedback goes wrong because the message wasn't good enough. But when you look closely at what actually derails feedback conversations, you see a different story. It's not the absence of information that trips us up. It's our belief that information alone is enough. This belief has a name: **the information fallacy**.

The information fallacy is the mistaken belief that if I simply give you the facts, you'll understand them, absorb them, and take the right next step. It assumes that objective information creates automatic clarity, learning, or change. If only humans worked that way.

In real life, information is filtered through a person's worldview, biases, emotions, level of self-awareness, identity triggers, relationships, stress, culture, and context. Information doesn't travel in a straight line. It gets interpreted, bent, filtered, reframed, and sometimes rejected before it ever lands.

All non-assertive feedback approaches are especially vulnerable to this fallacy because relying on information feels safe. It allows them to "share the facts" without stepping into the discomfort of directness, specificity, or accountability. Instead of saying:

- *"Here's the behavior I observed."*

- *"This is the impact."*

- *"Here's what needs to change."*

...they stay in the shallows:

- *"Just FYI..."*

- *"Something to keep in mind..."*

- *"People have said..."*

This isn't malicious. It's protective. It's a way to give feedback without feeling like they are giving feedback. But it creates confusion, not clarity, which is exactly the dynamic I described in my own experience receiving vague, passive comments that sounded positive but hid important criticism beneath them.

Why Information Alone Doesn't Work

Your people don't need more information. They need interpretation, context, meaning, and a clear path forward. The Ideal Process in this book emphasizes that productive feedback requires preparation, intention, observable behavior, impact, expectations, dialogue, and next steps.

Simply handing someone "the facts" violates almost every one of those steps. As the self-check in the course reminds us, effective givers prepare for emotions, ask for perspectives, clarify expectations, and confirm action and follow-through, not just deliver data. Without conversation, connection, and clarity, information becomes noise.

You'll see it everywhere:

- A leader emails a list of issues and considers the matter handled.

- Someone forwards a spreadsheet thinking the data "speaks for it-self."

- A manager tells someone, *"You came across as tough,"* but doesn't explain what that means or what needs to change, leaving the receiver confused, discouraged, and without actionable direction.

What's missing? Dialogue, specificity, and responsibility. Feedback givers often know something is off... but hope the receiver will piece it together on their own. That hope rests entirely on the information fallacy.

When we assume information equals understanding, we avoid necessary conversations, skip emotional preparation, withhold specificity, fail to check for interpretation, bypass accountability, and unintentionally create reactivity, defensiveness, or passivity in the receiver.

For organizations, the consequences look like inconsistent performance, unresolved issues, eroding trust, misalignment, stalled growth, and teams who feel like they must "read between the lines" and often guess wrong. Feedback is meant to unlock potential and transform performance, not require people to be mind readers.

How to Spot the Information Fallacy in the Wild

Listen for moments where someone insists:

- *"I already told them the facts."*

- *"They have the information."*

- *"People just aren't informed."*

- *"They'd understand if they would just read what I sent."*

These statements almost always signal an overreliance on data and an underuse of clear, explicit communication. Also watch for arguments or behaviors that reduce the issue to "just sharing the facts," ignore emotions, relationships, or context, and assume people process information rationally (spoiler: they don't). Also be on the lookout for behaviors that rely on passive communication instead of direct conversation and skip interpretation or next steps. If the entire strategy is *"I told them,"* you're staring straight at the information fallacy.

How to Counter the Information Fallacy

1. Bring the conversation back to behavior, impact, and meaning. Facts are only the starting point. People need help making sense of them.

2. Ask grounding questions: *"What did you hear from what I shared?" "How are you interpreting this information?" "What feels unclear or surprising?" "What do you see as the next step?"* These questions interrupt assumptions and build alignment.

3. Name the emotional, relational, and contextual factors. People aren't spreadsheets. Their reactions are shaped by fears, triggers, identity, and trust dynamics, which are the very areas we address in this program.

4. Follow the Ideal Process. The structure exists specifically to prevent this fallacy from derailing conversations. Facts become meaningful when paired with specificity, dialogue, expectations, action, time-

frames, and check-ins.

5. Remember skillpower + willpower. Often, a feedback giver knows what to say but lacks the will to fully step into it. Information becomes a shield, like an attempt to avoid discomfort while still "doing something." But as we've seen, skill without will is untapped potential and feedback avoidance is one of the most costly forms of that pattern.

The information fallacy is the belief that information is enough. But feedback is never just information. It is an interpretation. It is meaning-making. It is clarity, connection, and courage in conversation. It is the bridge between knowing and doing. It is the spark that creates change. The employees, teams, and leaders who avoid this fallacy are the ones whose feedback fuels growth, capability, and trust. Those are the leaders people remember.

If You're Stuck: Using DIP as Giver and/or Receiver

By now, you understand the common reactions to feedback and how easily conversations can derail when emotions, assumptions, or defensiveness take over. Even with the right intent and solid information, you may still find yourself stuck. The feedback doesn't land. The conversation goes in circles. Nothing changes. This is where Determine, Illustrate, and Propose (DIP) comes in.

DIP is not a replacement for the Ideal Process. It is a reset tool you can use within a feedback conversation when progress stalls, understanding breaks down, or resistance shows up. It helps you slow the moment down just enough to regain clarity, restore connection, and move forward productively.

You may need to use DIP when:

- The giver or receiver appears confused, defensive, or disengaged.

- You sense a mismatch between what you intended and how the feedback landed.

- Emotions are escalating, yours or theirs.

- You realize assumptions are being made on either side.

- The conversation feels stuck in explanation, justification, or silence.

In these moments, pushing harder rarely helps. Giving more information often backfires. DIP gives you a structured way to pause and re-engage the conversation with curiosity and collaboration rather than force.

DIP can be used by givers and receivers. As a giver, DIP helps you recalibrate when your message isn't landing as intended. As a receiver, DIP gives you language to slow the conversation down and seek clarity without becoming defensive. Most often, DIP is used in real time, right in the middle of a feedback exchange. It is especially useful when reactions such as passive rejection, active rejection, or passive acceptance begin to surface.

DIP stands for Determine, Illustrate, Propose. Each step is simple, and together they create forward momentum.

Determine: What is Happening

First, determine what is actually happening. This means getting clear on what you are observing, where confusion or resistance may be showing up, and whether the issue is about skill, will, expectations, or understanding.

As a giver, this might sound like pausing internally to ask yourself: Is this feedback clear? Is the reaction about the message, the delivery, or something else entirely? As a receiver, it may mean noticing your own reaction and acknowledging that something doesn't fully make sense yet. Determining prevents you from reacting on autopilot and helps you respond intentionally.

Illustrate: *Ask*

Next, illustrate by asking. This step is about inquiry, not explanation. Instead of adding more information or defending your point, you ask questions that surface perspective. Examples include:

- *"Can you share how this is landing for you?"*

- *"What part of this feels unclear or difficult?"*

- *"What are you hearing me say?"*

Asking creates space. It invites the other person into the conversation and reduces the likelihood of assumptions driving the outcome. This step aligns directly with effective feedback practices that emphasize listening and perspective-taking.

Propose: *Collaboratively Suggest*

Finally, propose by collaboratively suggesting next steps. This is where movement happens. Rather than dictating a solution, you co-create one. This might include exploring options together, agreeing on a small, testable change, clarifying expectations or support needed, and identifying follow-up or check-ins. The goal is shared ownership. When people help shape the solution, they are more likely to commit to it and act on it.

DIP works because it addresses both skillpower and willpower. It keeps conversations grounded in clarity and purpose rather than emotion. It shifts feedback from something that happens to someone into something worked through together. And it reinforces the idea that productive feedback is not about winning a point, but about enabling growth. When you feel stuck, DIP gives you a way forward without escalating tension or shutting the conversation down.

Chapter Three Key Takeaways: ACCELERATE

- Confidence comes from action. Practice is what turns awareness and learning into mastery.

- Productive feedback works best as a repeatable rhythm: before, during, and after the conversation.

- Use COIN to keep feedback clear, behavior-based, and actionable, especially when emotions run high.

- Receiving feedback well is also a process. Preparation, clarity, and emotional regulation help you stay engaged without defensiveness.

- When a conversation gets stuck, DIP (Determine, Illustrate, Propose) helps you reset, regain clarity, and move forward collaboratively.

- The information fallacy is the mistaken belief that simply giving accurate or complete information will automatically lead to understanding, acceptance, or behavior change. In reality, emotion, interpretation, and context heavily influence how feedback is received.

Reflection Prompts

Choose a past or upcoming feedback situation as you work through these prompts.

Create a COIN Statement

How might applying COIN have helped in a previous conversation? Or draft a COIN statement you could use in an upcoming conversation.

Assess Your Alignment to the Ideal Process

1. Where are you strong? Before the conversation? During? After?

2. Where do you need more skillpower?

3. Where do you need more willpower?

Identify 1–2 Areas to Improve

Based on what you've just seen: What matters most for your growth right now? What will you practice first?

Pick one or two improvement targets. Not ten. Not five. Just the ones that will accelerate your skillpower and confidence the fastest. Your next move is the most powerful one: **Apply what you know.** Practice. Experiment. Integrate.

You're not trying to be perfect. You're becoming skillful. And confidence will grow with every conversation. Next, we move into **PERPETUATE** — how to build habits, maintain growth, and make feedback a lasting part of your culture.

Chapter Four

PERPETUATE

Make Feedback Cultural

If you've walked through the first three stages — ACTIVATE, ELEVATE, and ACCELERATE — you've already begun the transformation from *"What the feedback?!"* to *"Wow, the feedback!"* But the real magic happens here.

The transformation becomes sustainable when feedback stops being an event and starts becoming the way you do things around here. It moves from something you "do" occasionally to something that flows through everyday conversations, projects, and decisions. That's what I mean by a feedback culture. A feedback culture is what happens when people share:

- The same language

- The same models

- The same expectations

- The same courage

It's where the ripple effect begins. This chapter is about that ripple and how to create it.

Feedback Culture Requires Both Sides of the Equation

A true feedback culture doesn't happen because one person on the team is great at feedback. It happens when everyone grows in both giving productive feedback (using the Ideal Process and COIN) and receiving feedback non-defensively (understanding their triggers and staying open).

Culture is not built by one heroic manager or one highly skilled individual. It's built through shared practice, shared language, and shared norms. When everyone understands:

- The three types of feedback (Appreciation, Coaching, Evaluation)

- The four approaches (Passive, Passive-Aggressive, Aggressive, Assertive)

- The assertive approach as the goal

- The COIN method

- The Ideal Process before, during, and after

- The four reactions to receiving feedback

- The triggers beneath those reactions

- DIP Method for Getting Unstuck

...that's when feedback becomes cultural. That's when feedback stops being scary and becomes normal, people start to see feedback as fuel instead of a threat, and performance and trust accelerate at scale. This is where the ripple becomes real.

The Ripple Effect: One Person → One Team → One Organization

Feedback culture grows through consistency, not perfection. It begins with one person — you — choosing to prepare, regulate your emotions, communicate follow-through, and receive feedback as data, not danger.

Every time you do that, you influence one conversation, one team dynamic, one project, or one performance cycle. Then something powerful happens. People begin to mirror it. They adopt your language and borrow your process. They use COIN because they saw it work. They ask for feedback because you made it safer and they give feedback because you showed them how.

This is how habits spread. This is how trust grows. This is how culture is built. If culture is "the way we do things around here," then feedback culture is "the way we give and receive feedback around here" — consistently, productively, and with respect.

During one of our **WTF-What The Feedback™** courses, a leader told me this story. She'd been dreading a difficult conversation with a team member. She knew it could get emotional. In the past, that alone would have led her to avoid it or rush through it. This time, she did something different.

She sat down beforehand and wrote out her COIN statement. She clarified the context, captured specific observations, and thought through the impact. She didn't script every word, but she gave herself a solid anchor.

Sure enough, when she started the conversation, the employee became emotional. *"In the past, I would have gotten swept up in that,"* she told me.

"This time, I went back to my COIN. I came back to the impact piece. Once I calmly shared the specific impact, she understood what I meant. The conversation shifted. It became less emotional and more productive."

That's the ripple effect in action: one moment, one choice, one person prepared with structure, language, and courage. And the tone of the entire interaction changed. Multiply that across a team, then across a division, then across an organization and you start to see why the way we give and receive feedback becomes culture, not just content.

Feedback in Special Situations: Extending the Ripple

A real feedback culture doesn't stop with "downward" feedback to direct reports. It shows up in every direction:

- Upward feedback (to your boss)

- Lateral feedback (to peers)

- External non-client feedback (vendors, suppliers, partners)

- Client feedback (customers, buyers, patients, end-users)

Great cultures make feedback available and accessible across all these relationships without fear, aggression, or avoidance. Let's walk through some of these.

Giving Feedback to Your Boss

Why It's Hard: Giving feedback to someone who evaluates you and signs your paycheck can feel risky. Even when your boss says, *"I want your honest input,"* power dynamics make the conversation feel delicate.

What to Be Aware Of: Before you speak up, assess the relationship. Does it support honest dialogue right now? Clarify your purpose and desired outcome. Prepare in writing (COIN is your friend here). Avoid assumptions about motives or intentions and stick to observable behaviors and specific impacts.

When Your Boss Asks for Feedback: This is a positive sign, but it doesn't guarantee they're ready to hear something hard. You can ground the conversation with a simple statement: *"Since you asked for my input, I want to share my perspective honestly."* If they become defensive, stay calm, stay respectful, and stay specific.

When You Want to Offer Unsolicited Feedback: Extra thoughtfulness is required here. Weigh the importance; is this meaningful enough to address? Ask permission first: *"Would you be open to hearing my input on a situation?"* Choose your timing carefully and stay composed if the conversation gets tense.

Key Takeaway: Upward feedback should be thoughtful, respectful, and strategic. Done well, it can actually strengthen trust and deepen partnership.

Giving Feedback to Peers

What to Be Aware Of: Peers usually don't have formal power over one another. That can make peer feedback easier due to less hierarchy or it can make peer feedback harder due to more potential awkwardness. Without clear role boundaries, people may worry about overstepping, damaging the relationship, or being seen as judgmental rather than helpful.

General Principles: Identify your purpose (*"Why am I sharing this?"*). Don't assume you know the whole story. Accept that your feedback is one data point, not the full picture. Deliver with partnership, not authority. Use COIN to keep yourself grounded:

1. **Context:** When/where is this happening?

2. **Observation:** What exactly are you seeing?

3. **Impact:** How does it affect you, others, or the work?

4. **Now/Next:** What could we do differently?

Peers respond best to clarity, positive intent, respect, and a collaborative tone.

Giving Feedback to Vendors / Suppliers

What to Be Aware Of: External partners may not have built-in trust with you yet. That makes feedback more sensitive and more necessary.

General Principles: Know your purpose (*"What outcome matters most here?"*). Don't assume they have full control over the issue. Avoid "fix this person" framing and acknowledge system or organizational constraints.

Strategies: Again, COIN helps focus on outcomes and impact, not blame. Check whether the problem sits inside or outside their control. Communicate your positive intent; you're aiming for better results together. Stay open to feedback about your role in the situation. Handled well, this kind of feedback strengthens the relationship while still driving performance.

Giving Feedback to Customers / Clients

What to Be Aware Of: Client feedback can feel the riskiest. If done poorly, it can impact business. Done well, it builds trust and elevates the partnership.

General Principles: Follow COIN and clarify your purpose. Avoid assumptions about their motives or expertise. Don't make the customer feel "wrong" or foolish and educate without being demeaning.

Strategies: If a conversation gets heated, propose taking a pause and revisiting later. Commit to following through and keep that commitment.

Here is one example from my own medical device days: If a surgeon wanted to use our product in a way that was outside of the product's instructions for use (which is a surgeon's prerogative), I might say, *"This is your call, of course. Could we agree that if the result we're both hoping for doesn't come to fruition, we'll revisit and consider the specified technique in the FDA-approved instructions for use?"* Clear. Respectful. Non-threatening. And it kept the relationship intact.

And I'll be honest. Feedback to clients is still the hardest for me. My default there can be avoidance. If you can relate to that kind of challenge, you are not alone. Upward and outward feedback often require the most willpower and the most structure.

Feedback Is a Team Sport

When teams learn feedback together, something shifts. Feedback becomes normal instead of exceptional. The team shares the same language and tools, and they use the same processes (Ideal Process, COIN). They support each other through the "icky, sticky" emotions and they bounce back from missteps more quickly.

In one of our **WTF-What The Feedback™** courses, we asked participants, *"What's something you used to think about feedback that you now see differently?"* Some of their answers:

"I used to think feedback only happened in formal performance evaluations. Now I see it's happening all the time — and it's fluid."

"I thought I was assertive in my feedback. Turns out, I was actually aggressive. I was direct, but it felt like a hammer."

"Identity got me. You gave examples, and I watched people respond exactly the way you said. I saw myself in those examples — and that shook me, because I pride myself on not being that person."

This is the power of shared learning and shared language. This is where the ripple starts to multiply.

When Skill Meets Will: The Breaking Point and the Breakthrough

Sometimes people gain confidence before competence. They walk away from training thinking, *"I'm good at this now. I'm assertive."* Then real feedback lands from a colleague, a direct report, or their boss, and they realize: *"I thought I was one kind of leader... but I'm showing up differently than I believed."*

That moment can create cognitive dissonance. It's uncomfortable. But that discomfort is not a sign the culture is failing; it's evidence that the culture is working. We cannot protect people from every uncomfortable realization. But we can support them, give them tools, practice with them, and normalize the "ouch" moments.

Habit-Building Through Community

To make feedback truly cultural, people need reinforcement, accountability, shared stories, and safe places to practice. That's why WTF includes alumni forums and communities, peer cohorts, group habit-building and challenges, practice labs, and debrief spaces.

In our WTF community of course graduates, people come back to share how a difficult conversation went or celebrate a breakthrough. They often ask for help with a sticky situation or come back to keep sharpening both their skillpower and their willpower.

Feedback isn't just a leadership task. It truly is a team sport. And it's far more energizing when you turn it into fuel together.

Why a Feedback Culture Drives Performance

The "soft stuff" here has a very real, hard-edged impact. Research across hundreds of companies shows that organizations with strong feedback cultures outperform those without them. In some analyses, organizations with robust feedback environments see:

- Up to 2x revenue and financial performance metrics

- Stronger retention of top talent

- Higher levels of alignment, role clarity, and engagement

- Better decision-making and adaptability

When people know where they stand, know how to succeed, receive clear and actionable input, and see their growth recognized, feedback becomes fuel. It unlocks potential and drives learning. It strengthens trust and collaboration and improves business outcomes.

In other words, **feedback culture = performance culture.**

Chapter Four Key Takeaways: PERPETUATE

- Feedback becomes powerful when it stops being an event and starts becoming the way work gets done.

- A feedback culture is built through shared language, shared tools, and shared expectations, not individual heroics.

- Culture grows through a ripple effect: one person modeling productive feedback influences teams, which influences organizations.

- Feedback must flow in all directions — downward, upward, lateral, and external — to truly become cultural.

- Preparation and structure (Ideal Process, COIN, DIP) make even difficult feedback conversations safer and more effective.

- When teams practice feedback together, it becomes normal, human, and growth-oriented, driving trust, performance, and engagement at scale.

Culture grows in community. You and your team don't have to do this alone. For additional structure, you can connect with me, engage in our course offerings, or attend the Friday Feedback Live! sessions. Even inside a single team, these habits can transform how you work together.

Feedback is not a moment. It's a muscle. It's a mindset. And with enough repetition, it becomes a cultural advantage that transforms relationships, teams, and organizations. You're ready to help build that culture. And the ripple starts with you.

Conclusion

From Fear to Fuel

If you think back to where we started together, we began at the edge of a bridge. On one side was uncertainty, the place where feedback felt uncomfortable, overwhelming, or maybe even a little scary. On the other side was possibility, the place where feedback becomes less of a threat and more of a tool... less of a burden and more of a catalyst.

You've crossed that bridge. You've walked the same path I've watched thousands of leaders, teams, and organizations walk when they shift from: *"What the Feedback?!"* to *"Wow, the Feedback!"* And you've done it step by step.

ACTIVATE: You uncovered what sits underneath your hesitation — the fears, the triggers, the wiring, the past experiences, and the emotional patterns that shape how you give and receive feedback. You learned that you can't change what you can't see, and that awareness is the first spark of growth.

ELEVATE: You built your skillpower. You learned the three types of feedback, the four approaches to giving it, and the four reactions to receiving it. You gained the language, clarity, structure, and intention to speak in a way that's both direct and human. You learned that assertive feedback isn't a personality type; it's a practiced skill.

ACCELERATE: You practiced the Ideal Process before, during, and after the feedback conversation. You strengthened the muscle of emotional regulation. You applied the COIN Framework. You learned what it feels like to stay steady even when a conversation gets sticky.

And you discovered the truth I return to again and again: Confidence doesn't come from being perfect. It comes from consistent action.

PERPETUATE: You saw how feedback becomes a culture through shared language, shared models, shared courage, and shared practice. You explored what feedback looks like in every direction. You learned how a single person — prepared, clear, and compassionate — can shift the tone of a whole conversation. And how one conversation can shift the tone of a whole team.

You saw how the ripple starts. And you saw how the ripple spreads.

If there's one message I hope stays with you long after you close this book, it's this: **The things we shrink from are often the very things that unlock our next level of growth.** Feedback, especially the feedback we fear the most, is often the doorway into a stronger version of ourselves.

Feedback is not a threat. It's fuel. It's the catalyst that accelerates your leadership, strengthens your relationships, sharpens your clarity, and increases your impact.

As you step off this bridge, I want to leave you with one invitation — the invitation I give every leader, every team, every person who chooses to work with me: Be the leader whose feedback creates more leaders. Be the person who chooses clarity over comfort, uses language that lifts people higher, and builds trust through truth. Be the person who helps people see what they can't yet see in themselves.

You now have what you need to cross the bridge again and again. And you will.

Because every feedback moment is a chance to practice. Every conversation is a chance to get a little clearer, a little steadier, a little more skillful. Your feedback can be the spark that strengthens teams, transforms relationships, and builds a culture where people thrive.

You are ready. Go lead with feedback that fuels. Take your feedback from "WTF?" moments to "WOW!" results!

Glossary

Essential Feedback Terms

- **Feedback Culture:** A work environment where feedback is expected, timely, and focused on growth. In feedback-rich cultures, conversations are used to build trust, clarity, and performance.

- **Feedback Triggers:** Emotional reactions that make feedback difficult to give or receive. Triggers can activate defensiveness or shutdown before the message is fully processed.

- **COIN Model:** A practical framework for giving feedback by describing the Context, specific Observations, their Impact, and discussing Next steps. COIN helps make feedback concrete and actionable.

- **Skillpower:** The learned ability to give and receive feedback effectively, including tools, structure, language, and practice.

- **Willpower:** The internal readiness to engage in feedback, even when it feels uncomfortable. Willpower determines whether feedback skills are actually used.

- **SKWILL-Power™:** The combination of skillpower and willpower working together. SKWILL-Power™ is what turns good intentions into consistent, effective feedback behavior.

- **DIP:** A simple, three-step process used when feedback conversations stall, feel unclear, or become emotionally charged. DIP helps either the giver or receiver slow the moment down, restore clarity, and move the conversation forward collaboratively.

- **Determine** – Clarify what is actually happening or being discussed.

- **Illustrate** – Ask questions or share examples to build shared understanding.

- **Propose** – Collaboratively suggest a next step or solution.

• **FEARS (Giving Feedback):** An acronym that captures the most common internal barriers that block giving productive feedback. FEARs reveal where willingness breaks down, even when skill is present.

- **Flak** – Fear of fallout, conflict, or negative reactions

- **Emotions** – Fear of strong emotional responses (theirs or yours)

- **Apprentice** – Fear of not knowing how to do it well

- **Retribution** – Fear of retaliation or negative consequences

- **Something Else** – Hidden or unspoken resistance

• **FEARS (Receiving Feedback):** An acronym that explains the internal barriers that make receiving feedback difficult or triggering. These FEARS highlight why defensiveness can arise and reinforce that receiving feedback is a learnable skill.

- **Feedback** – The word itself triggers anticipation and reaction

- **Emotions** – Strong feelings that interfere with listening

- **Awareness** – Discomfort with blind spots or new insight

- **Rigid** – Attachment to identity, habits, or existing beliefs

- **Skill** – Lack of skill in receiving feedback productively

Keep the Feedback Momentum Going

If this book helped you move from "WTF?!" to "WOW!", you don't have to stop here. Kim Baker offers two ways to continue building your SKWILL™ — the combination of skillpower and willpower that makes feedback productive, confident, and consistent.

WTF-What The Feedback™ Courses: *Giving Productive Feedback & Receiving Feedback Without Defense*

This expert-led training goes beyond theory and into real-world practice for leaders, managers, individual contributors, and teams. Participants:

- Assess their current feedback skillpower and willpower

- Identify personal fears, patterns, and blind spots

- Learn and apply a proven feedback process

Friday Feedback Live: *Free. Practical. Real-Time.*

Every first Friday, Kim hosts Friday Feedback Live! — a free, interactive session exploring real workplace feedback challenges. You'll gain:

- Practical guidance you can use immediately

- Live coaching and examples

- A supportive, judgment-free learning space

Continue the conversation! Learn more about **WTF-What The Feedback™** and join **Friday Feedback Live**: wtf-whatthefeedback.com